TOWNS
FACING
RAILROADS

TOWNS
FACING
RAILROADS

poems by

JO McDOUGALL

THE UNIVERSITY OF ARKANSAS PRESS
FAYETTEVILLE LONDON 1991

95 94 93 92 91   5 4 3 2 1

*This book was designed by Ch. H. Russell
using the Garamond and Optima typefaces.*

Some of the poems in this volume have appeared in *Bitterroot, Cow
Creek Review, Little Balkans Review, Louisiana Literature, Men and
Women: Together and Alone* from Spirit That Moves Us Press, *Midwest
Quarterly, New Letters, Poetry East, Tortilla,* and *Women Who Marry
Houses* from Coyote Love Press.

The paper used in this publication meets the minimum requirements
of the American National Standard for Permanence of Paper for
Printed Library Materials Z39.48-1984. (∞)

Library of Congress Cataloging-in-Publication Data

McDougall, Jo.
    Towns facing railroads: poems / by Jo McDougall.
        p.   cm.
    ISBN 1-55728-181-5 (alk.paper)
    ISBN 1-55728-199-8 (pbk. alk. paper)
    I. Title.
    PS3563.C3586T69 1991
    811' .54—dc20   90-11312
                                                       CIP

For Charla Jo and Chris
and
Duke and Cindy,
with me in some of these towns

Contents

TOWNS

FACING

RAILROADS

A Friendly Town

The chamber of commerce was glad to give me a map.
I saw a creek curving its southern border,
the Burlington Northern dividing east from west,
streets named Elm and Locust and Park
stringing it together.
Tonight, after moving in,
I walk to a place where one of those streets deadends.
I say to myself that being a stranger is not
knowing what lies behind these wide windows.

Burying My Mother

In the rooms of my mother's brain
by one, by two, the jiggers of light went out.
She climbed her apartment steps
a year at a time.

As I walk from her grave to my car
Napoleon's horses cut through snow
crossing Russia, Hannibal's armies
take the Alps, Stonehenge
is laid.

A Veteran of the War
Speaks of the Enemy

He glistens in our dreams.
We have no other enemies before him.
Our sons and daughters will have to make do
with lesser ones.
Ours, treacherous, foul, teeth rotting,
is what we want. We seek him daily,
listening for his cough, his swaggered breathing.
We devour him in thanksgiving.
Living long into our pensions,
we will lick him clean.

Snow Comes to Pittsburg, Kansas

The men in Harry's Cafe predict snow.
Seen in Fort Scott, they say, headed here.

Behind Willie Nelson a harmonica whines.
I think of a man I knew.

At the counter a woman taps her fingernails
against the formica.
At the sound the men fall silent.

Edge of America

In Kansas City, I'm shopping
the Sharper Image.
They've got the ocean on tape.
I step back ten years
to Maine, Mt. Desert Island, Thunder Hole
where, if you stand too close,
the ocean rages through a needle
and pulls thunder through your spine.
We hold each other, deaf and terrified.
Alone, safe and not far
from the exact center of the United States,
I think of the edge of America,
the gulls screaming around us like burning cats.

Small Town at Dusk

Cars on the bypass
move between places with restaurants
we have forgotten the names of.
Fireflies appear and disappear.
Night takes the sidewalks first
and then the marigolds and the sprinklers,
the children's skates.
Nothing argues with the ambling dogs
except the tree frogs and the occasional slamming
of a screen door.

A Stand of Pines

I knew I'd never stay on my father's farm,
hating the clay fields,
the corner stand of pines,
helping my father skin rabbits,
jacket and pants.
I left one night when the moon set.

Today as I pass a field, the patient figures of two mules,
memory stitches my skin
clean as the treadle Singer
clacking after supper into darkness,
clacking all night and into the rising chores.

Farm Wife

In this drought
pole beans will cycle early.
One day as she is driving to town alone,
the car dies on the highway.
The sounds of passing cars
are like the sounds children make
of the sounds of cars.
Her husband withers like the wheat.
He's been in town since yesterday,
drinking down the smell of dead cows.

How We Live

Walking out of Food 4 Less,
we see a car thrash over the curb,
heading for us like a speedboat.
The driver's face
is like the face of someone
stepping back from a table saw,
seeing that he has cut off his thumb.

In the Coffee Shops

of towns facing railroads
where the grocery and the P.O.
look across a highway at rails the trains forgot,
chatter clicks into silence
when somebody new walks in.
Then the folk of Jerome or Black Coffee or Start,
in Mama Dan's or Della's or The Mallard
light another cigarette.
Dishes continue to break
dreamily in the kitchen.

The Dress

Well, I'm her mother, and I cannot see it,
that kind of money for one more thing to wear
to the Frostee-Freeze. I guess I might have done
the same thing at her age but, hell, at her age
I was married and lived at the mining camp
raising two kids, the baby being her.
She put on the dress last night, a strapless thing,
slipping up from the bottom and down at the top.
She called Harold, the weenie boyfriend,
to come take her down to the Idle Hour.
Waiting, she crossed her legs and fluffed her hair.
I'll bet she wasn't dreaming of pukey babies
or a man who rolls away soon as he's done,
or once of herself, married willy-nilly,
tomtit for a husband and no money.
It cost what she makes in a week, but she's got to have it.

Farewell, Dusky Seaside

(a found poem, from Time, *June 29, 1987)*

Six inches from tip to tail,
the tiny brown birds made
their home in a ten-mile coastal stretch of marsh
near Titusville, Florida.
When development from nearby Cape Canaveral
began to encroach,
they stubbornly refused to move,
and their number declined
relentlessly.
Last week
the last known Dusky Seaside Sparrow
expired: Orange Band, a twelve-year-old male,
was found dead in its cage.

Scientists tried
to save the bird from extinction by cross-breeding it
with a hardier sparrow. But Orange Band died

before they could complete the job,
leaving five hybrid Dusky Seasides—one of them
seven-eighths pure.

Item, Page Three

I am waiting for the news that fits to find me:
    Woman Loses Arm to Brown Recluse
    Mother of Two Assaulted
    Resident Missing at Sea
    Poet Dies More or Less Old
never having written what she could hear
humming like crickets,
ancient and daily,
scattering before her feet.

The Visiting Assistant Professor
on the First Day Addresses Another Class
in Yet Another Town

She looks at the red-haired boy
in the third row.
She remembers a Cajun boy
in the last town
who sat on the low branch of a live-oak
the day she held class under the trees,
the day she read
"I Saw in Louisiana a Live-oak Growing,"
who dropped down from the branch after the poem
and dropped the class.

I'll Be Seeing You

World War II is slipping away, I can feel it.
Its officers are gray.
Their wives who danced at the USO
are gray, too.
Veterans forget their stories. Some lands they fought in
have new names, and Linda Venetti
who deserted the husband who raised cows
to run off with an officer
has come home to look after her mother
and work the McDonald's morning shift.
William Holden is dead,
and my mother, who knew all the words
to "When the Lights Go On Again All over the World."

At the Marriott

I dream of an old hotel,
tile floors cool in summer,
windows velvet draped against the heat
as I wait for the phone beside the bed to ring
and him to cross town.
The phone rings. A voice belonging to no one tells me
it is six a.m.

On Catalpa Street

At dusk, when kitchen-window light
settles on the grass like a picnic cloth,
he thinks of the town he lived in
when he was twelve,
the year his father died.
He remembers an evening after his father's funeral,
crossing the yards wide with dogs and mowers
toward the yellow light of the living room,
toward a baseball game on the radio,
a back porch that smelled like sour mops.
He remembers a man he had never seen before
sitting with his mother at the kitchen table,
his mother looking, turning toward him
as though he might have been the Perkins boy
come to paint the shed.

Buying a House

The people who live here have left
to let me look.
The real estate lady struggles with the key.
I see the half-bath, the den, the dining nook,
black shoes with cracks across the toes,
seed catalogs and toothpaste.
I should not be in this house.
There is something here I'm supposed to understand.

Homeplace

Awake while you sleep,
I tie and untie the strings of what went wrong:
the farm auctioned, my father buried in Minnesota,
you and I alone
in a rented room.

I remember my father when I was six
pushing open a gate on the farm road,
stirring the dust of August.
The locusts sizzling in the grass,
a hum of dragonflies hanging sleepy above us.

Driving Kansas

Skimming over macadam, Topeka to Hays,
I see a goat on the roof of a house
under a sky-blue sky.
Goat, hats off to you, I say
and raise my fist out the window.
The cold bites me like God.

Coyotes trot beside the highway.
I'm climbing into a land of limestone,
scattered tufts of grass,
no trees.
It is mid-afternoon.
I think of the
occasional house tonight
blinking itself awake as it drowns in the unending wheat.

Rooms

Whenever I see someone loading a car
with a Walkman, baskets, a rolled rug,
I think of what is left in the rooms
where people I have never met
argue or eat or pull on their socks.
Blindfolded, I could walk you through those rooms.
I could find, if I needed to, a needle I used once,
fallen between the boards.

Working Late in My Studio
on the Second Story

Sounds from the bypass drift up.
On the ground floor, a clock and the kitchen tick.
A cat yawns, pulling sleep out of the carpet.
My dead mother, who must be white as maggots now,
slips her voice under the front door.
I nod myself awake,
hoping I've been asleep.

Neighborhood

There is rage in the woman's voice
coming from a house close by.
Perhaps he is drunk again or home
smelling of women.
Her voice
shakes the catalpas.
The moon climbs over the town,
erasing windows.

Dead Child

It lived a week.
In the house, such fury.
The child's cries, chairs scraping, things boiling on the stove.
And always the child, its voice at chimney tops.

Then silences and whimpers.
The doctor's face.
The church,
the whisper of the coffin being wheeled out
like the rustle a last student makes
leaving the room on the last day of a semester.

Most of the Time

My mother sifts in my memory.
I can choose to see her
or not.
But last night as I tried to sleep,
she leaned across the bed and stared at me
and called me
somebody else's name.

A Bottomlands Farmer Suffers
a Sea Change

A man fits a key into the door of an office in Chicago.
Suddenly he remembers a plowed field.
He remembers the farm
before they took it.
He remembers walking its ditches,
flushing birds.

In a park across the street
pigeons scatter.
He hurries into the office
where a phone is ringing.

Fields

Driving the interstate from Little Rock to Conway,
I see rice growing in the fields.
It is green as crème de menthe.
The levees are dark chocolate.
I want to stuff the fields into my mouth.

Four P.M.

Now come A. J. Spence and wife
before bankruptcy court to pray
forgiveness of creditors, to say
how the hole in their lives grew
to take her mother's jewelry,
the 90 acres, and the cows.
Now come counsel and trustee;
now A. J. Spence and spouse
swear before God and furled flag
That then and now and here and there
they do relinquish and forsake
for any who come and any who care.

Marbles

I talk to my class about place.
Consider, I say, Tilbury Town, Gardiner, the Saginaw.
Some look at their hands
as if they are holding the words there
like marbles.

You appear in the door
from the Prairie Grove of our school days.
We go off to the playground and trade cats-eyes.

When I get back to the classroom
no one has noticed except maybe one student
who looks as though he lost the thread of my talk
or a pencil.

His Funeral

She despises the way funerals lie,
despises the baby's breath and wax leaves,
the undertakers
standing with their hands behind their backs.

She takes a seat directly behind the widow.
She remembers his body,
the motel rooms
and the way he fretted about hiding the cars.

The preacher is saying something about the children.
She wonders what the wife knew,
what happens to the body first
and how soon.

Surviving in Kansas

(for Richard Blum)

A man told me this
at a party in Topeka.
Bugs in Kansas, he said,
sleep on the roots of grasses.
There are no trees in Kansas.
Bugs go underground.
If you pull up the grasses
you'll find them.

Nearly certain this was a lie,
I asked him to dance with me.

Story

Decades ago
in a small, mad town,
there is an evangelist, soon to be my father,
with black, brilliantined hair.
Standing before the borrowed pulpit, shoes buried in sawdust,
he marries my mother with his eyes.
He leaves her before I am born,
taking his Bible with him
and her mother's brooch.

My daughters love the story.
At five and seven they are already turned
toward someplace else,
they and others like them raised in towns
of summer revivals, visiting preachers,
the one wide highway out.

Talking with You Long Distance

I get what I want.
You say it: It's your fault.

The wallpaper roses blur and fade.
A silver bowl on the table
has taken a skin of dust.

Packing

I want to come home.
I have been too many years in the rooms of others.
I am looking for
tall windows,
fireflies on the lawn.
Packing the last box again,
I watch the dark condense
across the grass.

The Day

You realize you'll remember it
as you leaf through a magazine
try on a hat
miss a plane.

He says he's leaving. You'll remember the way
he takes his shirts out of the drawer,
refolds each one.
The way your stomach turns
quick as you'd shake a spider
off a sleeve.

Children's Children

They watch from the silver ovals
I have caught them in,
boys and girls about to enter
the other side of time
although I speak to them often on the phone
and they send letters telling me
how, gently, with sweet apologies,
each in appointed turn begins to live
in days I'll see
on the backs of photographs.

Once in Winter

when snow fell light as ashes,
we walked Times Square.
Turning to kiss you,
I saw a man lie down in a doorway,
fitting himself
to the stone.

The Stump

When they lost the farm near Omaha
and their money,
the farmer's wife thought of it
as losing an arm.
The stump was a challenge.
It was, she said,
for the time being.
A healthy arm would sprout
if she were patient and wise and a hard worker.
But the stump healed smooth.
She watched things disappear:
the TV, the car, her teeth,
and still the stump offered nothing.
One night she began to understand
it would be with her always,
mean as a pig.

In the Home of the Famous Dead

The perfect visit. We pay and we go in,
the way we first enter a hospital room
except that we don't have to talk to anyone
and the men if they wear hats keep them on.
We know this is not the house they knew,
not the way they knew it, anyway,
when they were eating and laughing and having colds.
The best furniture has been removed, and the rugs.
What's left, the chintz and brass, is pissy stuff.
Still, there's a whiff of bacon in the kitchen.
We shuffle along beside the velvet ropes,
subdued. A small boy tries to cross under,
not yet afraid of dustless, perfect rooms.

Her Last Trick

Sit down and loosen your collar.
Let me take your coat.
Isn't this a nice hotel? We'll order wine.
I'm glad you like my dress. I always pretend
I'm invited to dinner with some rich old man
when I buy my clothes.
Well, here's to us.
You're married, right? Me, too. I got three children.
Hey, this is a business, like anything else.
That isn't what I meant.
There's something I want to tell you
before we start. This is on me.
You're surprised? Surprise is what we live for. Why else
would you be here?

The First Warm Day

Watching you take hammer and nails to your roof
is like seeing the shadow of my mother move
behind the screen door of a farmhouse on an Ohio hill
in April when trees stutter and tulips find
their old pattern and a clear creek moves
behind the gym of the high school where boys remember
spring and turn to their cars and highways
in search of girls on porches
protected by leaves that turn an even deeper green
because I am watching you take hammer and nails to your roof.

Remodeling

My mother fell flat on her porch the day it iced over
while she was gone to the store for a quart of milk.
I think it would be like that if she came back now
to hear us hammering on her house, whistling.

Growing Up on the Bayou de Glaises

Light would climb the walls of the sitting room,
wavering when a wind shook the water,
slipping in ribbons
across the only two pictures in the house:
Huey P. and Jesus.

Salesman

He sits in Bob's Grill,
the large gray leather case between his feet.
Unfolding the morning paper
he reads about a woman's body
found by the bypass,
her eyes, the sheriff says,
eaten by birds.

Humanities 113

A shoe, then a bucket at the beach, then a pet
slides through a dark slot
with no explanation from anybody.
Then a grandmother, then a friend.
I read from Thomas Hardy.
We are talking about
Literature and Death.
A girl on the front row yawns
stretching a slender arm
toward the tall boy beside her.

A Woman of Substance

Every day
his dead wife argues with him.
She argues and rocks and argues,
shelling peas.

Catalpa

(for Ann and Steve Meats)

When I am old and no longer able to remember
Shakespeare's Sonnet 73
or the names of my children
I hope I can call up when I want to
one catalpa bloom
balanced on the toe of my shoe.

Blessing

My neighbor hangs out the morning wash
and a storm dances up.
She strips the line,
the children's pajamas with the purple ducks,
her husband's shorts,
the panties she has hidden under a sheet.
When the sun comes out
she comes back
with the panties and the sheets, the shorts and the pajamas.
This is my ritual, not hers.
May her husband never stop drinking and buy her a dryer.

Upon Hearing about the Suicide
of the Daughter of Friends

Something called to her that Sunday afternoon, perhaps,
that she could not name.
You and I cannot name it, drawn to each other
by this news.
The young cry when they feel it
breathing beside them.
We may know it sometimes through its disguises,
say the sound of a car at two a.m.
grinding to a stop in a gravel drive.

To Her

I get up
from the cold bed,
open the door.
Someone with his hand at my back
pushes me into a room with a bed
where I am sleeping.
The woman in the bed will not wake up
although I beat on her chest
a long time.

Night Flight, Delta #481

We are rising up from Boston
heading for Bangor, Maine.
The flight attendant's smile
hangs before us.
A tube and a mask make circles in the air.

Once, in New Orleans, on Decatur Street
you drew yourself into a ring of chalk.
You danced to the skittering music from Mollie's Bar,
clicking the change in your pockets like castanets.
You stepped over the circle and disappeared
into the crowd.
I have looked for you—
by rivers,
in depots, on loading docks.
A man on skates,
a man bending to pet his cat,
a man running across a darkening street

is finally you.
He is not.

I turn out my reading light.
Pretending to touch your arm
I touch the window beside me,
cold as it passes through the stars.

They Agree to Call It Off but Then

She fixes a drink and forgets where it is.
She thinks how soon
others will bring her drinks of water
and smooth a blanket over her knees.
She hears the neighbor's children after school,
the thinning traffic.
She leaves a message on his machine:
Meet me in Wichita.
Wear the yellow shirt.
Answer your phone.

Dropping a Line

Six months have passed
and no word.
I am playing hopscotch on the page.
I skip everything I need to tell you.
If I cross a line or step on a stone
I am lost. I will not get into Heaven.
Therefore, I do not say Come back,
it is dark.

I send you this letter
without a line you can use.